STARTING SOCCER

Helen Edom & Mike Osborne

Mike Osborne is a Senior Lecturer at the University of Reading

Editors: Lesley Sims & Harriet Castor   Designer: Martin Aggett
Illustrator: Norman Young   Photographer: Chris Cole
American Editor: Peggy Porter Tierney

Contents

2 About soccer
4 Using your feet
6 Dribbling
8 Passing the ball
10 Farther and faster
12 Using your head
14 Getting the ball
16 Beating your marker

18 Goalkeeping
20 More about goalkeeping
22 Playing as a team
24 Playing fairly
26 Playing eleven-a-side
28 Smaller teams
30 Keeping fit and healthy
32 Index

Soccer boots and kit donated by Puma UK

About soccer

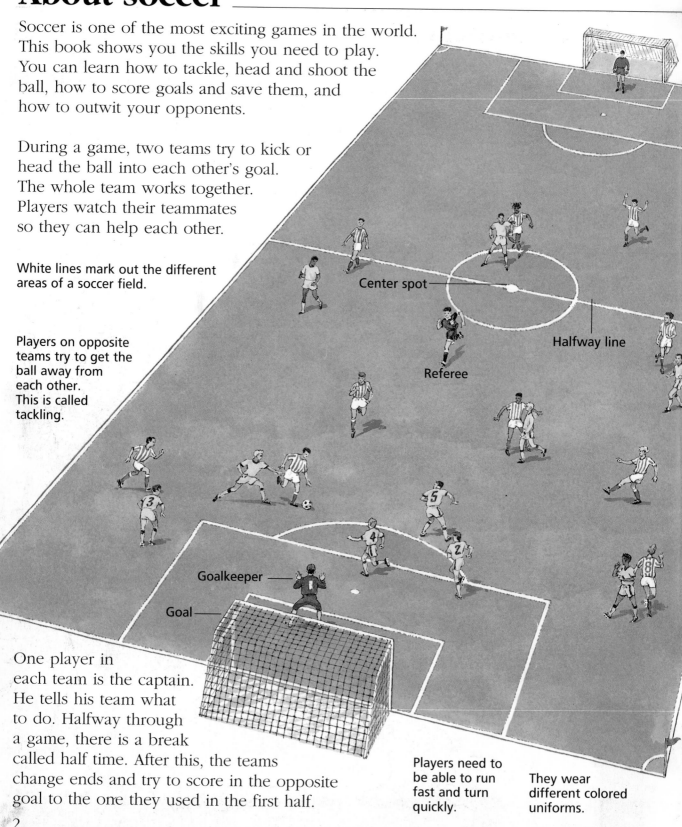

Soccer is one of the most exciting games in the world. This book shows you the skills you need to play. You can learn how to tackle, head and shoot the ball, how to score goals and save them, and how to outwit your opponents.

During a game, two teams try to kick or head the ball into each other's goal. The whole team works together. Players watch their teammates so they can help each other.

White lines mark out the different areas of a soccer field.

Players on opposite teams try to get the ball away from each other. This is called tackling.

Center spot

Halfway line

Referee

Goalkeeper

Goal

One player in each team is the captain. He tells his team what to do. Halfway through a game, there is a break called half time. After this, the teams change ends and try to score in the opposite goal to the one they used in the first half.

Players need to be able to run fast and turn quickly.

They wear different colored uniforms.

What you need to play

The first thing you need for soccer is a ball. You can buy one in any sporting goods store. Most soccer balls are made of plastic. They come in different sizes. You can buy a smaller, lighter one to start with.

Shoes for playing on grass have cleats on the bottom. These help to stop you from slipping.

To practice, wear comfortable clothes and non-slip shoes. For a game, you will need soccer shoes. There are different kinds of shoes for playing indoors and outdoors.

You can play soccer in any safe, open place away from roads.

Using your feet

Unless you are a goalkeeper, you will mainly use your feet to make the ball do what you want.

You can move the ball with different parts of your foot. Try with your toe, heel, sole, the instep and the outside. Do this with both feet.

It's easiest to make the ball go where you want if you use your instep. To make the ball go a long way, kick it with the top of your foot or "laces".

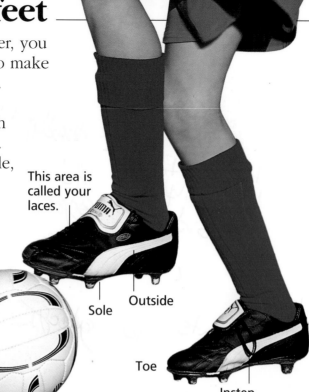

This area is called your laces.

Sole

Outside

Toe

Instep

Heel

Using your laces.

Using your instep.

First kicks

Use your instep.

Imagine a line around your ball, halfway down. To make the ball go straight and low, kick it on the line.

The ball was kicked here.

If you kick the ball below the imaginary line, it will fly up into the air. This kick is harder to aim.

If one foot is weaker, give it extra practice. It is very useful to be able to kick the ball with either foot.

Close control

You need to be able to control the ball really well, or other players will take it away from you. These activities will help.

Start by rolling the ball around with the sole of your foot, any way you like. Try this with each foot in turn.

Keep this leg relaxed.

Hold your foot steady on the top of the ball. Then roll the ball to the side until your foot touches the ground.

Go back the other way, until you touch the ground on the other side. Try not to wobble.

Do this with each foot. Make sure that your foot touches the ball the whole time.

Juggling

Throw the ball this high.

Use the top of your foot.

1. Throw the ball into the air. It should only go about as high as your head. Let the ball bounce once.

2. As it rises, kick it gently into the air. See how many times you can kick it before it hits the ground.

Players also use their chest or legs to control the ball. See if you can keep it in the air with your thigh.

Dribbling

Dribbling, or running with the ball, lets you get into a good position to kick to a teammate or score a goal.

Keep the ball still, to begin with.

Using your instep.

Using the outside of your foot.

This opponent has stolen the ball.

1. Standing still, tap the top of the ball with each foot in turn. Try to do this without looking.

2. Now move with the ball. Nudge it with the inside and then the outside of your foot.

3. Keep the ball just ahead of you, so you can see it and watch for other players.

Don't let the ball get too far ahead of you. Otherwise another player may reach it before you.

Dribbling races

Mark a spot with a coat. Try racing to it and back. See how fast you can go. Remember you must still keep control of the ball.

Then put some coats and bags in a line. Try to zig-zag the ball in and out of them. Use the inside and outside of each foot to make the ball go different ways.

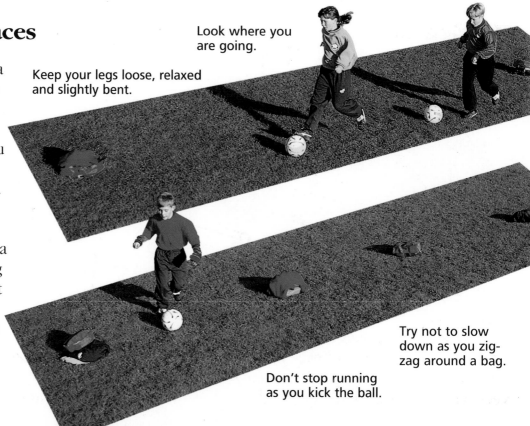

Look where you are going.

Keep your legs loose, relaxed and slightly bent.

Try not to slow down as you zig-zag around a bag.

Don't stop running as you kick the ball.

6

Dribbling tip

When you can control the ball, practice dribbling around an opponent.

Try changing your speed too. Dribble around your opponent, then sprint away.

Watch out!

Keep the ball under control so you can turn or stop quickly.

Both players can give signals.

This is a game for two. It helps you to practice looking out for other players while you are dribbling. Both players take a ball and begin to dribble. They must keep an eye out for each other.

At any time, either player may put up a hand. The other one must stop. One of the players may also point in any direction. Right away, the other player must turn in the direction pointed.

Passing the ball

One very important skill is passing the ball to other players on your team. This helps to get the ball nearer to the opponents' goal so that one of your players can score. The better your passes, the more chances your team will have to score.

Put your arms out to help you balance.

Short pass

It's easiest to aim with the inside of your foot.

When you pass, remember to aim the ball carefully. Shorter passes are more accurate than long ones.

Put one foot alongside the ball. Keep that foot facing forward. Turn your body a little to the side.

Kick the middle of the ball with the inside of your foot. Let your leg swing up as the ball moves.

Stopping the ball

When someone passes the ball to you, move your foot back as the ball hits it.

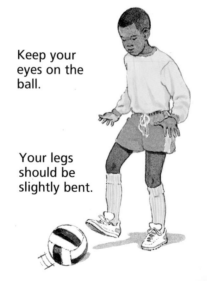

Keep your eyes on the ball.

Your legs should be slightly bent.

Your heel should be lower than your toes.

Moving your foot back like this, stops the ball from bouncing off.

This is called cushioning the ball.

Another way to stop the ball is by "wedging" it.

As the ball reaches you, lift up your foot and trap the ball under your toes.

8

Improving your aim

Ask a friend to stand a little way away. Pass the ball to each other. See if you can pass it with just two touches, one to stop the ball and one to pass it back. To make it harder, put two coats between you. Try to pass the ball between the coats.

Passing game

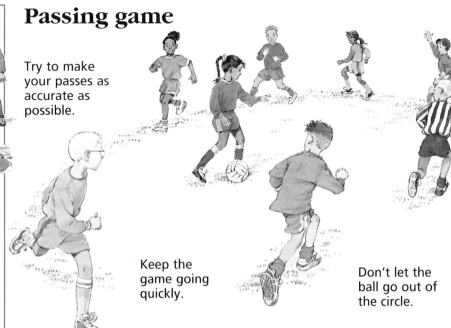

Try to make your passes as accurate as possible.

Keep the game going quickly.

Don't let the ball go out of the circle.

In this game, one player has the ball. The rest jog around her in a big circle. Then someone in the circle raises a hand. The player with the ball passes to him.

The player who has just passed the ball joins the circle. The new player with the ball dribbles into the middle and gets ready to pass to someone else.

Aiming at the goal

If you are near the goal, you can score using the side of your foot. Aim the ball away from the goalkeeper.

Low shots can be hard for the goalkeeper to reach.

Farther and faster

This page shows you how to put more power behind your passes.

Try to place your non-kicking foot alongside the ball.

Keep your leg moving after you have kicked the ball.

To kick the ball harder and farther, use your laces. This is useful for long passes or for scoring goals.

Start behind and to one side of the ball. Run up and kick it as hard as you can with your laces.

Kick with your toe down. Keep both legs slightly bent. Let your leg swing up after kicking.

Scoring practice

Try this exercise with friends. One person passes and the other shoots. The others roll the balls back.

It's best if you can use several balls.

Passer

Receiver

Shooter

Receivers roll the balls back to the passer.

The shooter stands 15-20m (16-22yds) from the goal. The passer passes the ball just in front of the shooter. The shooter runs forward and kicks the ball into the goal. Try to shoot without stopping the ball first. Take turns at being the shooter and the passer.

Stopping high balls

Using the top of your foot.

Using your thigh.

Push out your chest to meet the ball.

Sag back to cushion the ball.

Powerful passes may bounce, or come up high against you. You can use different parts of your body to stop the ball.

Remember to cushion the ball (see page 8). Bring your foot or leg down as the ball lands, to stop it from bouncing away again.

You can use your chest too. Spread your arms and stick your chest out. Sag back and downward as the ball touches you.

Two-touch game

In this game, you can only touch the ball twice in a row. If you touch it a third time, the ball goes to the other team. Try to cushion with your first touch and pass with the second.

You don't need a marked-out field to play this game, but it helps. In the game below, the players are using the circle on a full-size field to mark out the size of their playing area.

Using your head

If the ball is high in the air, you can use your forehead to send it where you want. This is called heading. It uses your neck muscles a lot so you must warm up before you try it.

Warming up

Push your forehead against your hand. Try to stiffen your neck muscles.

Tilt your head and push it against your hand. Do this to each side.

Drop your chin and roll your head slowly from side to side.

Heading practice

Use a fairly soft ball at first.

Grit your teeth or you might bite your tongue.

Push your elbows out to the sides.

Heading the ball is called a "header".

1. Hold the ball in both hands. Pull your elbows back and out to the sides. Push your head forward.

2. As your head touches the ball, let go of it. Stiffen your neck and push the ball with your forehead.

Throw-head-catch game

Stand in a triangle with two friends. One of you throws the ball to another, who heads it to the third. He catches it and throws it for the first player to head.

Heading the ball.

Continue like this around the triangle.

This player is ready to catch the ball.

Heading for a goal

You may get a chance to score a goal with a header. Try to head the ball down into the goal. This may make it harder for the goalkeeper to save.

A long header

A long header is useful to send the ball well away from your goal. Jump up to it, arching your back.

Heading game

You can play this game with two teams of three or more players. Head or throw the ball to each other instead of kicking.

Push your head and body forward so you hit the ball in the middle of your forehead.

Hit the bottom half of the ball. It will rise over the heads of the other players. Always remember to keep your eyes on the ball.

You can only score goals by heading the ball into the goal.

Getting the ball

Trying to take the ball away from another player is called tackling.
You must get the ball without tripping the other player or using your hands.

Marking

A marker stays close to an opponent and watches the ball. If it is passed to her, he tries to steal it before it reaches her.

Jockeying

When you jockey your opponent, you keep about 1m (1yd) in front of him. It slows him down and he may make a mistake.

Tackling

It is easiest to tackle someone if you start to one side. This forces the person to change direction.

Bend your knees and crouch slightly over the ball.

Try to kick the ball just before your opponent does. You may need to flick the ball over his foot.

Move away quickly.

Make sure you know what you are going to do next. Be ready to dribble, shoot or pass to another player.

14

Piggy in the middle

Three or four players pass the ball back and forth to each other. The "piggy" stands between them and tries to get the ball. If she does, one of the others takes a turn in the middle.

Piggy in the middle gives you passing and tackling practice.

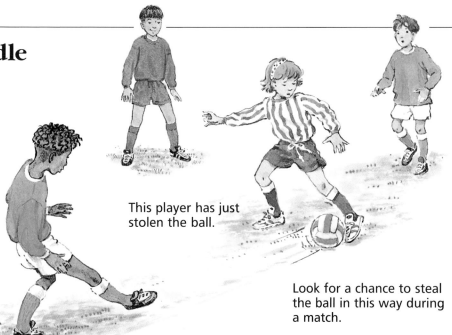

This player has just stolen the ball.

Look for a chance to steal the ball in this way during a match.

Tackling game

Use coats or bags to mark out the square.

Watch out in case someone sneaks your ball away as you tackle another player.

Mark out four corners of a square. Each of you dribbles a ball inside the square. At the same time, try to kick someone else's ball out of the square.

If your ball goes outside the square, you must drop out of the game. The winner is the last player left.

Sliding tackle

Sometimes soccer stars kick the ball away with a sliding tackle. Don't try this. Only very skilled players can do it without injuring themselves.

While this player gets up, the other player has a chance to take back the ball.

15

Beating your marker

If you have the ball, players on the other team will try to take it away from you. Here are some ways to get past them without losing the ball.

Sneaky moves

It looks like you are going this way.

You actually go this way.

Sprint away quickly.

One good trick is to pretend to go one way, but then go another. First lean as if you are going to move one way.

Your marker will move to block you. As soon as he does, shift your weight the other way and run off past him with the ball.

Your marker is now off-balance. This gives you time to get away. This trick is called wrong-footing your marker.

Pretend pass

Teammate

The marker thinks the pass will go to your teammate.

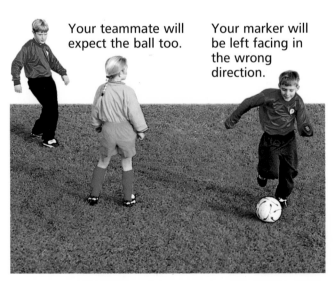

Your teammate will expect the ball too.

Your marker will be left facing in the wrong direction.

Another trick is to pretend that you are going to pass the ball to a teammate.

Your marker moves to block the pass. As she does, quickly run past her.

Crab alley game

Mark out an alley with pairs of coats like this. There is a crab (defender) by each pair.

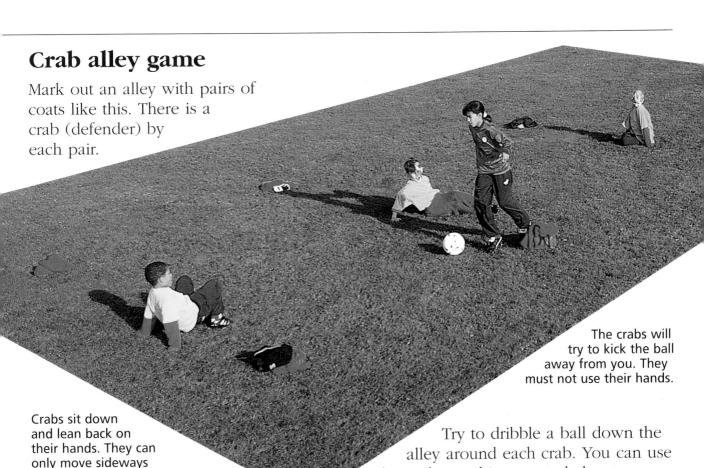

The crabs will try to kick the ball away from you. They must not use their hands.

Crabs sit down and lean back on their hands. They can only move sideways between their coats.

Try to dribble a ball down the alley around each crab. You can use the tricks on this page to help you.

Disguised kick turn

Your opponent is left standing.

1. Pretend that you are about to kick the ball straight ahead of you.

2. Instead, lift your foot over the ball and flick it just behind you.

3. Now quickly turn around and take the ball the other way.

Goalkeeping

If you are a goalkeeper, you have to concentrate and act quickly. You can either catch the ball or knock it away. If you catch it, your opponents can't kick it again.

Holding on

To see how good you are at holding the ball, pick it up and clasp it against your chest. Then do a forward roll still holding it.

Catching safely

Spread your fingers out.

High catch

Low catch

Keep your thumbs close together for a high catch. Let your little fingers touch to pick up a low ball.

Gloves help to protect your hands.

Goal shots are powerful. As you catch the ball, pull it into your chest to stop it from bouncing away.

This goalkeeper has just scored an own goal.

When you save the ball, you must keep hold of it. If you drop it behind the goal line, it's a goal.

Catching circle

You can practice catching with this game. One player throws the ball and then calls a name. The named player has to be quick to catch the ball.

Then the catcher throws the ball and calls out another name. You can make the game harder by using two or even three balls at once.

High and low

Sometimes you need to jump up to catch a high ball. You will go higher if you take off from one foot.

You may have to dive for the ball. Try diving from your knees, then try it from a crouching position. Keep your eyes on the ball the whole time.

This shows a goalkeeper diving and jumping for the ball.

Trapping the ball

Your legs can stop the ball if it slips through your hands.

Keep your knee and heel together or the ball may run through.

You can also use your chest to stop the ball.

If the ball is rolling slowly you can bend down and pick it up. Remember to keep your feet together.

If the ball is rolling faster, turn your feet sideways and bend down on one knee to catch it.

You can use your body as an extra barrier. If you miss with your hands, you will still stop the ball.

More about goalkeeping

Once you have saved the ball, you must make sure the other team does not get it again. Throw, roll or kick it to a teammate. Do this quickly before your opponents guess where you are sending the ball.

Kicking

To kick the ball a long way, drop it gently from waist height and kick it with your laces.

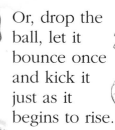

Or, drop the ball, let it bounce once and kick it just as it begins to rise.

Rolling

If a teammate is nearby, bend down to roll the ball. A low ball is easier to control. Look out for markers though.

Throwing

A thrown ball goes more quickly. Bend your elbow and push the ball forward.

To throw the ball farther, take your arm all the way back. Keep it straight as you throw.

Choosing the right player

Don't send the ball to a player who is being marked. A marker may manage to take the ball away from him.

Try to look for an unmarked player, or a player who has run around their marker into a clear space.

This player is marked.

When you throw, aim the ball as accurately as possible.

This player is unmarked.

Pushing the ball away

Sometimes you can't reach the ball fast enough to catch it. Try to push it away from the goal with the palm of your hand. Using the bottom of your palm puts more power behind it. Push the ball off the field. If you don't, the other team may get the ball again before you are ready to save it.

Push the ball around the post, or over the bar.

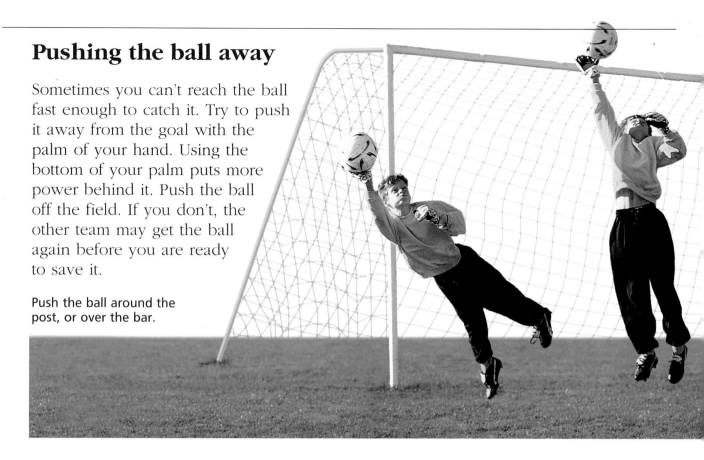

Coming out of the goal

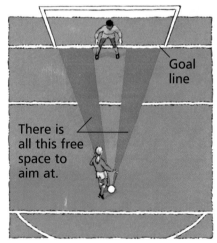

Goal line

There is all this free space to aim at.

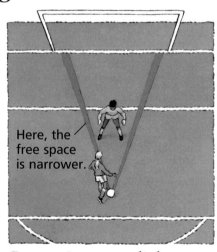

Here, the free space is narrower.

Try not to stay too near the goal line. If you do, you leave more room for players to shoot the ball past you.

By coming out a little, you can reach the ball more easily, wherever the attacker shoots it. There is also less space to aim at.

Be careful not to come out too soon or too far. This will give the attacker a better chance to get the ball over or around you.

21

Playing as a team

Soccer is a team game. It is as important to help a teammate get or keep the ball as it is to get the ball yourself.

Forwards and defenders

Before the game, players decide where they will play on the field. Forwards stay close to their opponents' goal, so that they can try to score.

Defenders stay near their own goal. They try to stop the other team from scoring. Some players stay in the middle, ready to help both forwards and defenders. They use the wings to get around the other team.

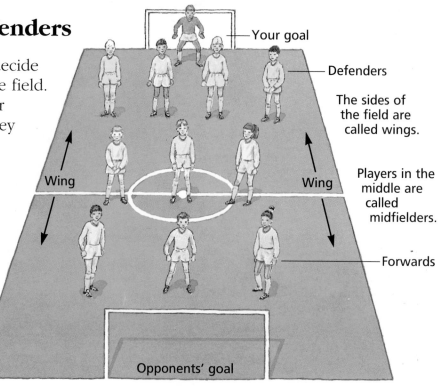

Your goal

Defenders

The sides of the field are called wings.

Wing

Wing

Players in the middle are called midfielders.

Forwards

Opponents' goal

Wall pass

Here's how to outwit an opponent. As a challenger tries to get the ball, one player passes it to another on the team.

The challenger turns to the player with the ball. The first player then runs around the challenger into a clear space.

Now her teammate can pass back the ball. This is called a wall pass because the ball goes to and fro as if it is bouncing off a wall.

22

Evading a challenger

If a team mate is being challenged, it may be risky for him to keep the ball. Make it easy for him to pass to you.

Be careful the challenger is not between you and your team mate. If he is, he will easily block the pass. It helps to shout to your team mate, so he knows where other players are.

Remember, a short pass is more likely to go to the right player.

This player is safer to pass to.

Here the challenger is in the way.

Cross-over play

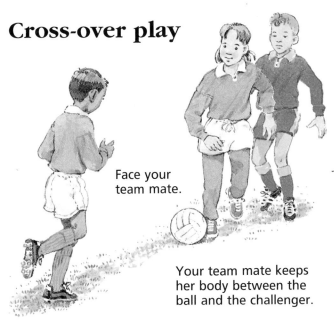

Face your team mate.

Your team mate keeps her body between the ball and the challenger.

This trick helps a team mate who is being challenged very closely. The pair of you run toward each other, until you are just passing.

Your team mate kicks the ball into your path, with the side of her foot. Run toward the ball until it crosses your path. Then dribble it safely away.

Playing fairly

Rules help to make soccer safe and enjoyable. If you break a rule, the referee will give the ball to the other team to kick. This is called a free kick.

The referee will blow a whistle and hold out his arm if he sees a rule being broken. If the player continues breaking rules, the referee may send him off the field.

Fouls

Breaking a rule is called a foul. Kicking, pushing or tripping a player, or touching the ball with your hands (unless you are the goalkeeper) are all fouls.

If the tackler here kicks the player's leg and not the ball, this is a foul.

Direct and indirect free kicks

Free kicks are taken as close as possible to where the foul happened. Opponents can try to stop the ball, but they must stand at least 9m (10yds) away. There are two kinds of free kicks. With direct free kicks, the person with the ball can shoot straight at the goal.

Direct free kicks are for serious fouls. For less serious fouls, the referee will give an indirect free kick. The kicker cannot score right away. He must pass the ball to another player before a goal can be scored.

This player is taking a direct free kick.

The line of opponents in front of the goal is called a wall.

Penalty kick

If a serious foul happens near the goal, the referee gives a penalty kick. A player shoots the ball from a spot called the penalty spot.

Only the goalkeeper can try to stop the ball.

The goalkeeper mustn't move forward until the ball is kicked.

Being offsides

This rule applies only at the moment when the ball is kicked to you. You must not be the closest person to the goal you are aiming for. Two or more players on the other team must be level with you or closer to their goal. If not, you are offsides.

The goalkeeper counts as one opponent.

If the ball is kicked to her, this player is not offsides.

If the ball is kicked to this player, she is offsides.

If you are offsides, the referee will give an indirect free kick to the other team.

Playing eleven-a-side

In most professional games, there are eleven players on each team. A game lasts for 90 minutes, with a ten or fifteen minute break at half time.

The player on the right has kicked off, passing the ball to a teammate.

Kickoff

There is a kickoff at the start of a game, after half time, and every time a goal is scored. At the start of a game, a coin is tossed to decide which team kicks the ball first.

After a goal, the team that didn't score gets to take the kickoff.

The referee puts the ball on a spot exactly in the middle of the field.

Then the referee blows a whistle and one player kicks the ball.

Going off the field

Lines on the long side of a field are called sidelines. On the short sides they are goal lines. If you knock the ball over a line, the referee stops the game.

The referee then gives the ball to the other team. How the game starts again depends on whether the ball crossed a sideline or a goal line (see page 27).

Referee's assistant

A referee's assistant stands outside each sideline. He helps to decide where the ball crossed a line or if a player was offsides.

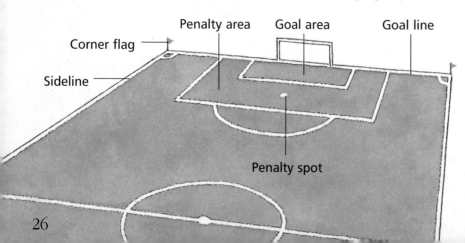

Corner flag

Sideline

Penalty area

Goal area

Goal line

Penalty spot

Throw-in

Use both hands.

Keep both feet on the ground.

Stand where the ball crossed the sideline, but outside it.

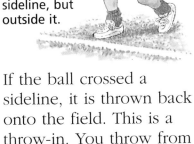

If the ball crossed a sideline, it is thrown back onto the field. This is a throw-in. You throw from behind your head.

Corner kick

A corner kick is taken from the corner circle.

If you knock the ball over your own goal line, the other team has a direct free kick. This is called a "corner".

Goal kick

The ball must be still when it is kicked.

Goal area

If you knock the ball over the other team's goal line (but it isn't a goal), they take a goal kick from the goal area.

Free kicks and throw-ins

Make the most of any free kicks and throw-ins you have. Sometimes take them quickly. This gives the other team less time to prepare.

Always try to plan your moves. Many teams score most of their goals from free kicks.

If the other team has a throw-in, guard the thrower and mark any player he is likely to pass to.

The player with the ball is aiming over the head of the challenger.

Smaller teams

Soccer can be as much fun to play with small teams. You can have a good game with any number of players from three to seven-a-side. These are called small-sided games.

Small-sided games are like eleven-a-side games but are played on a smaller field. This means they can often be played indoors.

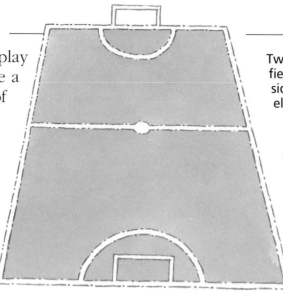

Two of these smaller fields can fit side-by-side onto an eleven-a-side field.

The goals are smaller than usual.

There are semi-circles instead of boxes in front of each goal.

Keeping the ball low

To keep a ball low, kick it with the inside of your foot.

Usually, in small-sided games, the ball must not go above head height. If you kick it too high, the other team gets an indirect free kick.

Kickoff and timing

Instead of a kickoff, the referee drops the ball between two players, one from each team.

The game also restarts like this if the ball goes over the sideline.

Small-sided games can be short. Each half may only be six minutes long. If the score is equal after the second half, the game can go on until another goal is scored.

28

Goal area

The semi-circle in front of each goal is called the goal area. Only the goalkeeper is allowed inside it.

Goalkeepers outside the goal area must obey the same rules as the other players. They can only kick or head the ball.

Outside the goal area, the goalkeeper must not touch the ball with his hands.

Scoring goals

Goal area

There is no offsides rule in small-sided soccer. You can pass to anyone, but you can only shoot at the goal from outside the goal area.

Penalty shoot-out

The teams have the same number of shots.

Each team may have three, four or five shots each.

In a tie game, there is a penalty shoot-out. Each team has a set number of kicks. Only the goalkeeper can defend. The team with the most goals wins.

Keeping fit and healthy

Soccer can be hard work. Always warm up your muscles before you play. Muscles pull on bones to move them. Warming up makes muscles stretchy so they work more easily. If you don't, you might strain or injure them.

Start by jogging forward.

Turn around.

Then jog backward.

Warming up

Start warming up by walking briskly to the field. Next, try some gentle jogging. Swing your arms as you jog. After a few minutes, do the other exercises shown here.

Ankle circles

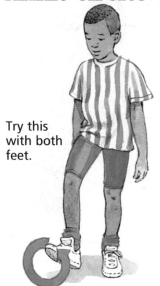

Try this with both feet.

Lift one foot off the floor. Draw a circle in the air with your toe, first one way and then the other.

Calf stretch

Keep your back leg straight.

You should feel a stretch here.

Point both feet forward.

Keep both heels on the ground.

Put one foot behind you. Bend the other leg until you feel a stretch. Count to eight, then change legs.

Groin stretch

Always stretch gently.

This stretches muscles at the top of your legs.

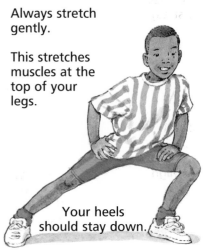

Your heels should stay down.

Stand with your feet very wide apart and bend one knee. Hold for a few seconds, then change legs.

30

Side stretch

Looking up helps this stretch.

Reach up with one hand as high as you can. You will feel a stretch down your side. Count to eight, then stretch the other side.

Neck and shoulders

Remember to do the warming up exercises for heading the ball (page 12).

Lift your shoulders up to your ears, so you're hunched up. Then let them drop back down. Do this three or four times.

Thigh stretches

Try to keep your back very straight.

Push your bottom out behind you.

Feel a stretch in the back of your thigh.

Count to eight and change legs.

Put one leg out straight in front and bend the other knee. Lean forward until you feel a stretch.

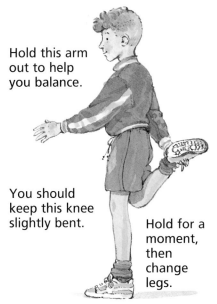

Hold this arm out to help you balance.

You should keep this knee slightly bent.

Hold for a moment, then change legs.

Stand on one leg. Bend the other one up behind you. Grip your ankle and gently pull your foot up.

After play

Your muscles are very hot after playing. Put on warm clothes so they don't cool down too quickly.

You will probably be hot and sticky. If you can, take a warm bath or shower after the game. It will also help to relax your muscles.

Index

ball, 3
ball control, 4-5

catching circle, 18
challengers, 22, 23
corner kick, 27
crab alley game, 17
cushioning the ball, 8, 11

defenders, 22
disguised kick turn, 17
dribbling, 6-7

eleven-a-side, 26

forwards, 22
fouls, 24-25
free kicks, 24-25, 27
    direct, 24
    indirect, 24-25

gloves, 18

goalkeeping, 18-19, 20-21, 29
goal kick, 27
goal scoring, 9, 13, 29

heading, 12-13

jockeying, 14

kickoff, 26, 28

marking, 14, 16, 20,

offsides, 25, 29

passing, 8-9, 10-11
    pretend pass, 16
    short pass, 8
    wall pass, 22
passing game, 9
penalty kick, 25
penalty shoot-out, 29
piggy in the middle, 15

referee, 2, 24, 25, 26, 28
referee's assistant, 26

scoring practice, 10
shoes, 3
small-sided games, 28-29
stopping the ball, 8, 11, 19

tackling, 14-15
team play, 22-23
throw-head-catch game, 12
throw-in, 27
two-touch game, 11

warming up exercises, 30-31
wedging the ball, 8

Useful addresses

The Football Association
16 Lancaster Gate
London W2 3LW
England

United States Soccer Federation
1801-1811 S. Prairie Avenue
Chigaco, IL 60616
USA

Australian Soccer Federation
Sydney Football Stadium
Driver Avenue
P.O. Box 175
Paddington
NSW 2021
Australia

Canadian Soccer Association
237 Metcalfe Street
Ottawa
Ontario K2P 1RS
Canada

New Zealand Soccer Association
P.O. Box 11357
Ellerslie
Auckland 6
New Zealand

With thanks to:-

Soccer players: Joshua Bamford, Carl Brogden, Thomas Chalk, Sarah Fuller, Sonia Gill, Jenna and Samuel Lanyon-Hogg, Alexandra Littler, Kristian Olloman, James Pearce, David Pugh, Aaron Ripley, Ben Tipton and Edward Wisson.
Husborne Crawley Lower and Fulbrook Middle Schools.